Amryl Johnson

Tread Carefully in Paradise

Cofa Press – Coventry

Published by COFA PRESS, 1991
12 Canal Buildings, Leicester Row, Coventry CV1 4LH

British Library Cataloguing in Publication Data
Johnson, Amryl
Tread Carefully in Paradise
I. Title

ISBN 1 873471 01 7

Printed in Great Britain by
Warwick Printers, Warwick, England.
Typeset at The Page Factory, Coventry.

The poems in this collection have all appeared previously in *Long Road To Nowhere,* Virago Press, and *Shackles - Long Road to Nowhere,* Sable Publications.

Contents

Blowing in a Random Breeze

Whitewash the face of hunger
When all the features have been removed
paint on the smile, the laughing eyes
Show the tourists what they want
But not too close
Behind the grinning facade are slums
which rob the people of all dignity

A fan screen blowing in a random breeze

The trail of dust which sifts
up to the dirt road leads to where the earth
is stone and breaks the hoe. The seeds
cannot be coaxed in rain which
does not come
You walk away with callous
hands, defeat

A fan screen blowing in a random breeze

The fishing boats come in
The sea has drawn a seal between itself and them
There is nothing to be said
Each man goes down to drown in silent thoughts
The only movement is their eyes which stray
towards the mouths of disappointed
family and friends

A fan screen blowing in a random breeze

This is no door which swings half
off its hinges and yet protects you still
This is the worm–holes of decay and rot

It creaks with every stir you make
  groans with every breath you take
  moans with every current of air
trapped by your weary feet
In a random breeze it fans the overflowing
cesspit of poverty and want

In a random breeze it weeps

For a Sister

You got it lady!
Hit it
bang
centre
Is that what it is?
        you
        me
de boat ah we
paddling that same
damn canoe
bailing for all we worth
fighting sharks
        predators
who try to wrap their
        arms
around our defiance
battling plankton
who only want to come in
        and shelter
for a little while
like we
        you
        me
de boat ah we
outta de raging sea
So where the calm
        Dee
    where the calm
when the still
silent sea
stopped raging
so long ago?
Stopped
        You
        me
    de boat
            ah we
still
fighting
the monsters
which are
no longer
there

Shackles

The dividing line is slim
It exists no more
Ironic laughter rippled
through the breeze
the night
a leaf
as cold as iron
blew against my feet
clung to my ankle
shackled dead in my tracks
catapulted back
in time
to taste
the icy thorns
of sorrow
Sent me stumbling
like a lunatic
to a bar
Drink up!
the man said
It's closing time
I choke
on the dregs
of my ancestry

The Birds Must Eat Also

Stretching up to take the fruit
I see the cobra
swaying in the branches
As bright as gold
its tongue is a clutch of diamonds
flicking among the guavas
serpenting between the needles
of the pineapple
My eager fingers are rusty hinges
I dare not touch
But the faintest echo of a drum growing
louder by the minute reminds me
that I was here
once before
I was here among the
shaddock, the oranges and the plums
                among the
cashews, the pomeracs and the tamarinds
I came down when the gash in my side
like a man's fist
and the pain which slashed furrows in my brain
brought me from the fields
                        to my knees
This soil is my blood
its fruit nurtured on my flesh
There can be no sin in this
no sense of guilt
no shame
This land is mine
My body vibrates to the frenzied drum
which becomes my own heartbeat
I tear fruit from the branches
The ones I cannot reach
a barrage of stones sent tumbling
to the ground
Hands and mouth sticky from the juices of
mangoes and sapodillas
I am in paradise
Pain like a dull reminder
paralyses my wrist
rips at the scars
The fruit falls

The cobra swaying in the trees
gold in the sunset
waiting in the branches

but there is no serpent
It is only your jewelled hand
stretching out to steady me
lifting my face to meet your eyes
so soft and understanding
you told me of the things
I forgot
to remember

There were so many

Your gentle voice still follows as
head bowed
I walk away
At the gate
your last words are sealed in
with the drying mask
and gloves which will hold
me rigid until they crack

'–at the very least
the birds must eat also'

Far Cry

Loud voices in the market place
barter with wily vendors in head ties
The ample hips sway to an awareness
of their sensuality
The touch and feel of their own
uniqueness
The memory plays tricks
and I saw them
                coming out of the frightened jungle
        still coming
                coming

in chains of bewilderment
Lost insufficient souls
chained to the yoke which
would be their hallmark for centuries
erasing from the memory of future generations
the boundaries of a continent
beyond which
existence and death
had not seemed conceivable
and where they would be
                coming with the impetus of the whip
        still coming
                coming

to fields where sweat never dries
and the question mark of selection
burns a charred and bitter trail
in your heart and understanding
Stranded in a horror where the spirit is trained
to cower and servility rewarded with a bone
fear is the hunter which traps you
in your skin
They found themselves
                coming to feel they were less than human
        still coming
                coming

to terms with the alien tongue
plunged into an alternative culture
The shut lips are a slash of silence
where anger is just one more sip
of the bile which foams ferments then
rises like a volcano you then swallow
lava flows down to the stream of degradation
until one day you found yourself
                coming with the first unsteady step

still coming
coming

through that tunnel of darkness
drawn to a light burning pale
Where it strikes with a faint glow
it hits the twisted gnarled labour
of your body distorted gestures of
freedom discredited by shapes which
still follow shadows of shackles on the wall
New found courage to turn from the power of
its glare habit of obedience and look at
yourself without feeling shame you start
coming to face the mirror
still coming
coming

to shake the dust from your elbows and knees
learn to stand straight before reaching down
to pick up the pieces with the will
to fit them together again trying hard to
accept there are sounds which time can
never fade
Moving with caution on the road to dignity
until your footsteps are firm and sure
You walk now with the lust to survive
and begin
coming to build your own foundations
still coming
coming

to lay the first willing stone of walls built
with nails which split wood
and knots which bend nails
Your house stands on unsheltered ground
where you scratch the soil which the
fowls search both looking for the same grain
of corn provisions of little
And the hills you are climbing are the same
hills you climbed but the timber on your back
makes your burden much less so you are
coming in search of more fertile land
still coming
coming

to find your children's hunger for knowledge
is the tool which is needed to chisel the future
The features of your destiny were carved in
reply to their search for a solution
Now the landscape of time has become your
dream of tomorrow and the violence which
erupted your vast solid earth to a clump

of small islands in the reshaping of
decades met you
          coming through the line of coconut palms
     still coming
          coming

to where the cars speed on the new highway
The concrete houses with electric kitchens
leave small space for doubt
and much room for indulgence
in swimming pools and hot and cold showers
but the uneven pace left so many behind
that a few with a particular brand
of awareness came to show their people
another road which found them
          coming towards the fire
     still coming
          coming

from the charred macabre chasms of consciousness
a sound like the scraping of dead bones
Too many lives too many fears
Too many years of too much suffering
Too much anger too much pain
blood and mutilated flesh
The strain and tension
wear of the centuries still tear
the islands can never lie still
          coming with hurricanes and earthquakes
     still coming
          coming

to bind the last few strands of a rope
bargaining hard for the clean break
and the laughter in the market place
ringing mocking and hollow is hushed
All heads turn to listen once again
to the sound which had them swaying their
hips but only one may feel the filaments
which tease the comprehension when she
finds herself
          coming when the drum mutation calls
     still coming
          coming

to gyrate on the streets
on Monday and
Shrove Tuesday

and be silenced
on Ash Wednesday

The Coconut Grove

In the late evening mist something fell
among the shadows to rise and steal
like urgent wisps
through the undergrowth
I felt it
harsh and bitter
No breath can warm this memory
It can only spin the thoughts which cause
fear to stir and clutch the senses
Citadels so tall
against the stars
no longer sway
or lift a branch to comb the sky
The demon force which
juggled
bricks and roof-tops
left them deaf as well as blind
They cannot tell it is a gentle wind
that comes to circle the grove
and go on its way
They can no longer tell the difference
between the hawk and the dove
the hunter and the quarry
the hurricane
                    and the breeze
These headless phantoms now stand
like monuments
to mourn
a deluge

Panorama from the North Stand

I am drawn towards one conclusion
This is nothing to do with a steelband competition
This is where the hibiscus and the humming–bird
lie down and roll over in sweet contentment
My crumpled senses are assailed
I am bludgeoned into submission
sucked into a vortex of music and pleasure
as wave after wave of intensity pull me from
the beach of self awareness
I cannot swim
I cannot pull against the tide
I cannot hope to win any fight against this baby
I must go down and drink deeply from
the vat of wonderment
Drunk with disbelief
I lie prostrate
numbed by the experience
Fragments of conversation burst upon me like bubbles
  Well, boy, boy, I never knew dat!

This is nothing to do with a steelband competition
This is an experience of Bacchanalian proportions
A procession of iceboxes and pots
initiated the proceedings
The umpteenth rum and coke is placed in my fist
Another plate of food is shoved under my nose
I hold my stomach
  You must be joking!

  But girl eat, nah! Yuh go get tin!

This is nothing to do with a steelband competition
This is a lesson in living
I am amazed at their capacity for enjoyment
I am humbled by their generosity
I am dwarfed by their magnanimity
I am envious of their spontaneity
I am –
Am I the only person looking at the band?
Everyone else has his back to the stage
hailing his friends
  Cedric, Merrill, Look meh!

This is nothing to do with a steelband competition
Co-existence in an atmosphere so highly charged
I am carried sky-high on a bolt of electricity

set free from enslavement
loosened from my inhibitions
I may never need to take refuge there again
DJ music punctuates the steel orchestrations
A hot calypso favourite sends arms flying
voices raised in raucous rendition
  Oh Gard, oh!
  Oh meh Lard, oh!
  Oh Lard, oh!
  Oh meh gard, oh!

I could be wrong about this
With the precision of a well–oiled pendulum
like an orb which is thrown from hand to hand
the pivot of their attention swings
Catelli All Stars have taken the stage and
North Stand's enthusiasm knows no bounds
They are ecstatic
Amoco Renegades hold their attention
Invaders – Yeees
  but
when sections of Desperadoes caterpillar settle down
and start to play
it is a whole new ball game
Dumbfounded by the crowd's reaction
I turn to a friend
  What's wrong with Despers?!!

  We eh like dat tune!

My people are like the leaves of an evergreen
planted in the finest dawn
Nurtured on their own audacious extravagance
they are fresh and total

King of the Band

Between the iron, the steel and the ding-o-lay
I see
the king of the band
Only so high
but already a professional
in motion
A woman standing next to me
jabs me in the ribs
  Look, look nah! De boy really know how to dance
he costume.
The feathers and the sequins take on a life
of their own
You're swaying to the music
they doing something else
They're jamming

Cloaked in turquoise and purple
scarlet and the shades of wonderment
the colours do more than reflect the sun
they splinter the rays snatching at
globules of the melting gold like
voracious fire–eaters
then belch them back with the
same intensity
into the furnace of a
Caribbean afternoon
The process is a never ending one of
separation, absorption and expulsion

Martyr for the day
Your headdress is an ornate structure
of beaten copper studded with gems
A crucifix they must relieve you of
from time to time
Beads of perspiration run like rivulets
down your brows
leaving a pattern of spikes
like the crown of thorns
The paint and the glitter is
now smudged and dirty yet
you're still smiling bravely through
it all

For

the videos are on you
the cameras are on you
all eyes are on you
and the show must go on
Knowing this
you break into a dance which has them cheering
Impetus at you heel
you grind life into the moisture still
resting from the late morning rain
Steam rises from the soles of your shoes
For today
you are king
you have the world at your feet
For today
you are king
The world lies easy at your feet
For today you are king
The king of the band

The children's carnival is held on the Sunday before Ash Wednesday. It gives even a tot the chance to parade in a costume exotic enough to deem her (and/or him) queen (or king) of the band.

J'Ouvert

(The setting)

Morning is a conspiracy
in which the king
rules the roost
Beaked for a first crow
he is shocked off his perch
by the pulse
of a steel drum

Night stretched languidly
to transparency letting in
pinpricks of light
pulls herself together

The days the months
the hours are enough
time in which
to mislay tradition

Leapfrog
the order of things
Confuse
the laws of nature

This dawn
belongs
to the people

Magnetized by the
unreal hours between
darkness and light
we
the damed
come out
to frolic
free-
        dom
is a word
is a word
is a word
with body and soul
in mind

The people slaved for it
          now guard it carefully
             release it
                with liberation
             without reservation

                for J'Ouvert

J'Ouvert *(corruption of the French* Jour Ouvert*) is the early dawn revelry on Carnival Monday.*

J'Ouvert

(We ting)

So many people in de ban'
we movin' like sardine in a can
Calypso vibratin' in we head
we arm, we back right down tuh we leg

Such sweet music comin' from de pan
gain breath an' rise high up in de sky
A breeze whisper 'notes eh hah no right tuh fly!'
He lose courage and waft home back tuh we

Dis time we hol' every note de pan leggo
explore, stroke it 'til we know de way it flow
peel every layer from it dat we can
every note die happy in we han'

Is a dancin' army on de move
steppin' to de island's latest tunes
All shades o'folk in perfec' harmony
De battle groun'? A shared ecstacy

We eh hah no malice on we mind
Is not war is joy we aimin' for
tryin' to wring as much pleasure as we can
before is time to surrender to de dawn

Now more ah dem joinin' in de crush
Stan' still an' dey carry you along
Squeezin' into any small space dey see
holdin' any man or 'oman dat dey please

An' if yuh see how we prancin' we jumpin'
we shakin' we winin' every inch ah we body
as if single cell bindin' de ban'
sealin' de people in dis common unity

Yuh dohn dress up for J'Ouvert yuh dress dung
Put on old clothes an' some washicongs
De mood is yours to do what yuh please
Wear what yuh like an' yuh do it with ease

When you start to look aroun'
Yuh cahn believe de tings goin' on
All sorts ah nice interestin' surprise
as folks free up dey body as well as dey min'

Ah see some big big lawyer in town
wearin' a bra an' a see-thru night-gown
an' dem girls who always in de social column
caked in mud an' wan' smear we dung

Jab Molassie dem slippery beast
covered from head to toe in red grease
pointin' pitch fork tuh frighten de crowd
carryin' tin can an' dey beatin' it loud

It eh jus' we ban' in dis Bacchanal
Dey dancin' wit' other steel band like dey mad
an' dis fever ragin' in we blood
burnin' like a fire in we soul

De atmosphere in Port of Spain still wil'
wit' celebratin' we liberty in style
Is hours we evoking de spirit ah Carnival
callin' she tuh take charge when we done

Too much pressure from de side
now we steel band start to slide
is brute force pushin' against de metal frame
tuh guide we music back tuh centre lane

All curtains ah grey now pushed aside
as de sun slowly begin to rise
bathin' we in golden shafts ah light
de final dimensions ah delight

Dis abandon to pleasure is drawin' we
to one conclusion of unity
Freedom was bought wit' dis in min'
a full expression ah liberty
so
dey cahn take dis from we
J'Ouvert is 'we ting'

Washicongs: plimsolls

J'Ouvert

(Running down)

The mask slides
I am revealed
Waxed entrails of unity
glistening
ugly
Skulking
back
wards
into the sunrise
I shield my face
against its rays

They have no right
not them
the newcomers
just arrived
fresh
from their yawns
watching
we
weary
warriors
footsore
defeated
against our own excesses
turn tired eyes
towards home
longing
for a few hours
rest
before –

Papillon

You paraded
like a jewel set in the dawn
Transparent wings, precious, so fragile
offered themselves like a gift to the Gods
The rays of the mid-day sun mellowed
against two veils of brilliant yellow
Wavering in the breeze, struggling vaguely
against an almost resistable pull
you beat once, twice then bowing
your head, you slowly closed your wings
to remain silent and still
A leaf drifted down beside you

Descending in hoards
you were like a conquering army on the move
Stroked by a loving rainbow or
dipped in the corners of the night
you made your way along the concrete
field certain of victory
but you took the light
  you took the air
  you took our breaths
  you took my patience
in endless rows of display

  I don't ever want to see another damn
butterfly as long as I live!

Later,
I came to regret these words
Memories fresh and throbbing
still zinging through my head
I came to where the brilliance of your
colour lay mangled
trampled underfoot
barely discernable beneath the filth and the mud
Ravaged by fatigue
Three days without sleep
I also was a torn and ragged traveller
On an impulse
I fell to my knees and started to weep

Desolation in the streets of Port of Spain

River

(Carnival Monday)
I was not there
I only heard
about your bleached purity
as you stepped out to dazzle and stun
by your elegance
draining the colour from tradition
you came as one
remote in unity
distancing yourselves from uninitiates
like me
total in absolution
beyond reproof
superior by far to anything
on the road to salvation
opening eyes but not minds
disturbing concepts
of what is or is not
I did not see
I only heard

(Carnival Tuesday)
The corrupt virgins of your temple
rejoiced in their own shortcomings
mesmerized by the transparency
of a rainbow
And the woman was defiled
Innocence lost
clawed from
                the legend of a man
who scuttled in his own blood
and the mechanics of an idea
from a man of vision
Somewhere in that dream
state of hypnotic flow
magic screened the mirror
                        by which
the people could judge their
own actions

Flow river flow
Draw the prisms of colour from the sky

Shafts of brilliance shuddered to the surface
rippling the red down to the violet
and I who fear the turbulence
of all waters
feeling its presence swirling
to engulf me
would have drowned in ecstacy
gone down
in a whirlpool of
indigo, yellow and green
But I was torn between conviction and
envy
Excluded from the fantasy
I longed to be with them
wanted to be like them
and not just on the bank of the River
This was more than just Carnival
a band of revellers
This was something I could feel and
I could touch
I t was close and it was tight

I stepped in
knowing my fate
The danse macabre
And went down with the people
of the River

Shrove Tuesday marks the final day of the Carnival. The lull commences on Ash Wednesday. 'Papillon' and 'River' were Carnival bands of 1982 and 1983 respectively.

And Sea

They brought me here to be baptized
among the chicken bones
the tin cans and corroded vomit
to stain the whiteness of my gown
and test the mooring of my faith
with the environment of my awareness

River and Sea

There was a time when I would sit
for hours and watch
the people of the River
now at home in the sea
And then one day
the froth and foaming menace
seeped in to fill the furrows
and seal the lightly shuttered exits
of surprise
moistening by degrees the parched and arid grains
of reasoning
The sun opened every crevice of hell
letting in the stench
of rotting faeces
My stomach pushed upwards
I snatched my clothes to run, escape
is through the shifting sand which pulls you
back with every step
Claiming you
The waves still offering their treasures
lay them proudly on the beach
but the rags which bind your feet are no match
for the broken bottle which threatens your heel
And the shifting sands pull you
down into a well of your heritage
Naming you

No tourist comes here except by chance

The people's beach they named it
they claimed it
they deserve it

There was a time when I would sit
for hours and watch
the people of the River
lying easy in the sea
ecstatic in their pollution
And then one day
I said
no more

Granny in de Market Place

Yuh fish fresh?

Woman, why yuh holdin' meh fish up tuh yuh nose?
De fish fresh. Ah say it fresh. Ah ehn go say it any mo'

Hmmm, well if dis fish fresh den is I who dead an' gone
De ting smell like it take a bath in a lavatory in town
It here so long it happy. Look how de mout' laughin' at we
De eye turn up to heaven like it want tuh know 'e fate
Dey say it does take a good week before dey reach dat state

Yuh mango ripe?

Gran'ma, stop feelin' and squeezin' up meh fruit!
Yuh ehn playin' in no ban'. Meh mango ehn no concertina

Ah tell yuh dis mango hard just like yuh face
One bite an' ah sure tuh break both ah meh plate
If yuh cahn tell de difference between green an' rosy red
dohn clim' jus' wait until dey fall down from de tree
Yuh go know dey ripe when the lizard an dem start tuh feed
but dohn bring yuh force–ripe fruit tuh try an' sell in here
it ehn burglars is crooks like all yuh poor people have to fear

De yam good?

Old lady, get yuh nails outta meh yam!
Ah mad tuh make yuh buy it now yuh damage it so bad

Dis yam look like de one dat did come off ah de ark
She brother in de Botanical Gardens up dey by Queens Park
Tourists with dey camera comin' from all over de worl'
takin' pictures dey never hear any yam could be dat ole
Ah have a crutch an' a rocking–chair someone give meh fuh fr
If ah did know ah would ah bring dem an' leave dem here fuh s

De bush clean?

Well, I never hear more! Old woman, is watch yuh watching meh
young young dasheen leaf wit' de dew still shinin' on dem!

It seem tuh me like dey does like tuh lie out in de sun
jus' tuh make sure dat dey get dey edges nice an' brown
an' maybe is weight dey liftin' tuh make dem look so tough
Dey wan' build up dey strength fuh when tings start gettin' rough
Is callaloo ah makin' but ah 'fraid tings go get too hot
Yuh bush go want tuh fight an' meh crab go jump outta de pot

How much a poun' yuh fig?

Ah have a big big sign tellin' yuh how much it cos'
Yuh either blin' yuh dotish or yuh jus' cahn read at all

Well, ah wearing meh glasses so ah readin' yuh big big sign
but tuh tell yuh de trut' ah jus' cahn believe meh eye
Ah lookin' ah seein' but no man could be so blasted bol'
Yuh mus' tink dis is Fort Knox yuh sellin' fig as if is gol'
Dey should put all ah all yuh somewhere nice an' safe
If dey ehn close Sing–Song prison dat go be the bestest place

De orange sweet?

Ma, it eh hah orange in dis market as sweet as ah does sell
It like de sun, it taste like sugar an' it juicy as well

Yuh know, boy, what yuh sayin' have a sorta ring
De las' time ah buy yuh tell meh exactly de same ting
When ah suck ah fin' all ah dem sour as hell
De dentures drop out an' meh two gums start tuh swell
Meh mout' so sore ah cahn even eat ah meal
Yuh sure it ehn lime all yuh wrappin' in orange peel?

De coconut hah water?

The Unpaved Road

Bind the open thoughts
with logic and swallow
each word to
regurgitate it into sounds
which will make no waves
Make no waves
Unsure
hoping you may care to read
between the lines
Make no waves
The still and silent sea is at my back
Make no waves
The unpaved road is where
you still move wearily
out of reach
and my last words are impaled
on that thorn-racked hedge
still riding those tortured few seconds
as I tried to hold you
a while longer
You did not turn
Your reply was a single word
which fell
to become dust stirred
by your heels until
you were out of sight
I measured your farewell not in
the distance between your steps
and mine
but in what little you took
So much still haunts that unpaved
road which starts at my front door
And yet
the silent sea waits at my back
No waves
I turned to watch it move from turquoise
through all the tiny changes which
rendered it
slivers of silver like dancing glass
And still no waves
as I go down
tight-lipped and reticent
hanging on with fists of steel
like any marooned slave
clinging to the wreckage

Spices and Guns

(Grenanda–March 1983)

Brave New World
where the waves crashing against
the pock-marked black-scarred rocks
do not crumble the resolve
the determination of a people
where the streets of khaki and
boots beat the baking pavement

Among the island faces is a fever
of ease
nurtured on hope that the gently
bubbling cauldron will hold
enough resources for all

I did not understand so once
again I came to see
To see and learn

The green metal dominance
did not disturb my equilibrium
did not alter my concepts of what
is right or what is wrong
did not shock my sensibility

I was taken by surprise
The strength of the fragrance
the pungence of the nutmegs and
cloves overpowered me
left me stunned
A surge of expectancy had me
reeling with the impact
of realization
and a hope for the future
of those gentle people with
their friendly ways

Black Coral

Rare to this flesh-eating scenery
which devours the evening
at Morne Rouge
with a sun which sets
as if falling from the sky
you would stand with a mirror to your thoughts
deflecting the rays which bounced
off you
proud, exquisite Africa
Often
    I would watch
    as you stripped
    the coral
    curving its black form
    tenderly
    patiently
I wanted
    to bend time
    and take you
        take you
    back to your kingdom
One day
you came out of the sea
clutching a branch which was not
black coral
Smooth as ivory
it was naked as bone
You held it out to me
smiling
Taken aback
my gaze fell from it to you
                                it to you
and then back again
I thought of skeletons, piranhas
and your own shrinking will
I could not answer when you called
You called my name again
I did not turn
I walked away without
a backward glance

The urgency had gone
out
of the longing

Until the Next Time

I will put on
my overcoat
and tiptoe
through the ashes
of a love which took
so long
to die
And it is not my feet
you understand
but my arms
which feel the cold
Maybe in time
they will grow to know
the logic of my ways
and
still
these precious embers
        may melt my thoughts
        may warm my soul
        may keep me
in good stead
until
the next time

Nutmeg

A perfect
peach
round gold
velvet to the touch
unblemished
virgin
inviting
desire
slowly
a slit
hint
a glimpse to tease
attract
opening
releasing a scent
to draw attention
In time
the intent becomes obvious
no longer coy
bold
unashamed
spreading wider
reveals the ripped
tattered petticoat
Red
but still shielding
your smooth mahogany
Somehow
still waiting to be taken
and yet it
never comes to that
You do not wait
you give
release
your treasure
falls
Spent
but not discarded
Your empty womb
a shell which
bears the fragrance
the perfumes
of your labour
The price
so high

you never can
let go

You carry it
with you
to the end

The New Cargo Ship

They came out of the belly of their suffering
into
the new cargo ship
joyful
singing songs
drinking rum
radios blaring
on the sea
once their enemy
This boat is crammed
as it was then
Still travelling
            in transit
always in transit
And the young man who led
the rebellion is now
the old man
in the red shirt
high with fervour
singing wiht feverish enthusiasm
drunk on whisky
drunk with disillusion
The one whose stomach heaves
with every wave
was the one who threw
himself overboard when
he could take no more
A people on the waves
            of the waves
And where was I in all this?
Where was I?
A stranger sits
in a corner
sipping Carib
observing
listening
The outsider
And where was I in all this?

Where was I?
Was I even then the watcher?
Where did I stand?
Where was I in all this?
Where was I?
Was I –
   We here, boy! We here!
The voice slashes the link
weakening the chain even further
   We reach Tobago!
Forgetting the danger
I stand up
straighten my crumpled dress
and join the passengers
waiting
to disembark

How Do You Feed The Ghosts?

How do you feed those emaciated spectres
which rise from the trenches of near
forgotten battles
hungry for recognition?

How do you make the gouged-out mutilations
which cling to the brackish waters of
restless pools
whole again?

How do you nurture those thin grey threads
which suckle along your nerve endings
during the open
hours of darkness?

How do you fill the sound which echoes like
slow footsteps through the black
slime of a never–
ending tunnel?

How do you feed the ghosts?

The Wheel

A wheel
of absurd dimensions
A thing of dire consequences
cane rust caked and molassed
lies in the rut where the tributaries
of history flowed
When all the rivulets merged
it should have vanished
with the evening
melted back into the past
It stood silhouetted against the sky
drawing in the pain and suffering
began to turn
revolving knowledge of how it was
Pressure building up inside my head
forced its own path
Steam hissed through the channels
pierced for escape
The night noises came too soon
bringing with them sounds so different
from the ones I thought to hear
The wheel
vibrates as all
who knew their place in life
are pulled towards this field
magnetic hold
Emancipated souls hang
grimly hub to rim
locked in a web
of fate
Equal now and free
planters and slaves
fight to control
their circle of destiny
Their only claim of space
in time
Possession
of
the wheel

In Tobago a gigantic wheel, now reclaimed by nature, is almost all that remains of what was once a sugar mill.

The Rockley Boys

Chattel houses
moved
from servility
to a thrust for revenge
white flesh on
hot beaches
give it to them man
that's what they
came here for
do it good and
they'll come back
for more

Chattel houses
spawned
alert boys
who seize their chances
easy money
easy pickings
go through her purse
even if she's looking
take what you can
they owe us man
she won't complain
she knows the game

Chattel houses
schooled
smooth operators
who know all the angles
if you tell
we'll come and find you
there'll be no safe place
while you're on the island
look under your bed
before you turn out the light
check all the windows
make sure they're bolted tight

anachronistic evil

unmoored vessels of stagnation
with dubious foundations

little wonder
they go
so readily
with any
determined wind

Tread Carefully in Paradise

Stunted in the cotton mills where their forefathers fight
was lost in threadbare bitterness
of fruitless labour some
rumoured to the penal colonies
they knew the branches did not stretch
as far as privilege
so did not feel an obligation
to the debt
Tread carefully in paradise
I warned before they came
Victims have no name or face
just traits of his own race
Friends back home are neither black nor white
What is there to fear? We're all the same
and share a common enemy the one who tries
to keep you pinned beneath his boot
They should have know that punishment
bears no relation to the crime

Hard work and sacrifice would be rewarded by
two weeks on sun–filled golden beaches
Sweet dreams have no resemblance to despair
when suspicion is not your forte
Trust is a measure you judge
by your own yardstick
but not here where the guideline
is only stranded fury
Tread carefully in paradise
my words got lost behind
the baring of the teeth
mistaken for a smile

Rape need not touch your body
just your senses
violate the most sacred sanctuary
of awareness
ravaged by words spat with violence
from hate foul mouths
when sport encountered
efforts of resistance
I could not tell the tear
stained cheeks and empty purses
Tread carefully in paradise
you did not listen to my warning

Anger and disgust clamped
my lips from speaking
I turned my eyes in shame from those which searched
mine for more than just a reason
full face into the sun's
one eyed burning glare
Its spotlight fell again
on one solitary footprint
still blatant on the beach
after all these hundred years
The void which all the island's rains
and storms can never hope to fill
A marooned fate which I as one
will never manage to escape

The blame is mine
I should have said much more
than
tread warily in paradise

Now I will need to lead them
step by step
back along that precarious footing
to try and make them comprehend
why their ordeal can never count
for any more than just
one grain of sand

Peanut Vendor

Nuts! Nuts!
Frrr-esh peanuts!
Reach fer yuh money!
Be quick! Be hasty!

Lady lookin' so pretty in de green dress
Stop, take a peep and see fer yuhself
Ah promise ah sellin' only de bes'

Nuts! Salted nuts!
Fresh an' crisp!
Put dem to yuh lips!
Dey better dan a kiss!

Girl, ah tell yuh dese nuts hot from de fire
Ah does roas' dem meself wit' love an' desire
Is de trut' Yuh tink ah is some kinda liar?

Nuts! Nuts!
Get yuh roasted nuts!
Good an' fresh!
Hot's de best!

Dou-dou yuh know yuh lookin' real nice
Earrings, shoes an' yuh hanbag jus' right
Tell meh, nah. Yuh wan' come home tonight?

Fresh nuts!
Roas' today!
So warm dey go burn yuh clothes!
So fresh dey sweeter dan any rose!

Darlin' ah love yuh as soon as ah see yuh
Ah hah a car, meh own house an' a lotta property
Leave yuh husban', ah sure ah go make yuh real happy

Stop fer yuh nuts!
Dohn be in a rush!
Ah sellin' out fas'!
Meh stock wohn las'!

Ah eh know wha' wrong wit' all yuh women
Ah talkin' nice an' ting an' yuh still eh answerin'
An' worse dan dat, it look like yuh eh wan' buy meh

Nuts! Nuts!
Salted nuts!
Fresh an' tasty!
Be quick! Be hasty!

The Immortelles

The immortelles are in bloom

A dart of memories softened the wrinkles
lifting her early years out of dusty crevices
where innocence was edged with grief
and pleasure the play and echoes
of children's laughter
taking her along a distant road
with narrow, now unfamiliar footholds

I went as a pilgrim to where they dusted
the hillside with embers of fire
and found them infinite
Taking courage from the sun
they offered a path of brilliant flecks
but I could not trample this
carpet of willing blossoms

'Mother to the cocoa'
On another island a woman balancing
a sack of nutmegs as if it was a crown
and her cutlass as a sceptre pointed
to where the immortelle
shielded the precious crop
keeping it cool in its shade

Somewhere else by chance
I saw a river where
a host of tiny lilies
shielded from the light curved
against a giant boulder
A flood of orange flowers
gently stirring with the wash

In L'Anse Formi I found
the fruit of this great tree
Rustles of secrecy among the green
Its nest like pendants
the Yellowtail tempts
with the merest hint
A glimpse of feather

I returned to tell of what I had seen
and she sat once again on giant shoulders
A small child with a dream of forever
reaching up to capture the blossoms which
will never fade and I can still recall
my mother's smile when I
by chance remarked

The immortelles are in bloom

Shrapnel

Bomb blast

reminders of an early warning system
which responded too eagerly
came too close to its target
caught me unawares

Shrapnel
I carry the pieces in my brain

Detonation

one iron will moving firm against another
rigid pride which will not yield
triggered by a feather light blow
impact is a noisy, messy break

Shrapnel
ripping your confidence to shreds

Shattered

pulling down the shutters and the blind
but not quick enough to escape the razor
sharp image which punctures the lens
The grey flecks are in the mind's eye

Shrapnel
piercing the crippled vision

Tension

plucking chords which should ease
and stroke the fevered will are
so highly charged they string taut
The bow which glides now hacks
like a saw on fettered bars

Shrapnel
splintering the emotions

Shell-shock

dazed uncertain tattered rags of disappointed
dreams limping home to pick up the remnants
weighted down by scales tipped out of favour
and exploding reality

there will be no medals pinned on me

Qu'est- ce Qu'elle Dit?

Qu'est-ce qu'elle dit?
The answer as always
Rien
Je n'ai rien dis
It comes again
Qu'est-ce qu'elle dit?
I told you
Nothing
I did not say anything

High above the window
the plastic coated meshing
designed to keep intruders out
obscures my view of the avocado tree
Branches heavy with flowers
its leaves so dense
they keep the sun at bay
The Keskidee bird calls
The three notes curve like a question
Caught unawares looking down
at your reflection
the cry becomes an indictment
Where an angle of despair meets
the sharpness of the wind
it cuts to transpose the plaintive
kes-ki-dee?
kes-ki-dee?
to
qu'elle dit?
qu'elle dit?
The flock may come
The interrogation begins
where are you going?
what did you say?
how will you get there?
what did you say?
what will you find there?
what did you say?
what did you say?
what did you say?
Grip the wire bars and scan the sky
Follow your vision across to the
coconut trees
You can hear but never find them
unseen tormenters
And
there are questions for which
you may never
find
answers

The Loaded Dice

Throw de dice, girl, throw!
Dey say is pure chance wha' bring we here

Throw de dice, girl, throw!
When dey divided Africa, who getting where

Throw de dice, girl, throw!
Is now we legacy to pass from han' to han'

Throw de dice, girl, throw!
If we lucky life good, if not we in a jam

Throw de dice, girl, throw!
Is a risk all ah we hah to take

Throw de dice, girl, throw!
Is your turn to roll an' know yuh fate

Throw de dice, girl, throw!
We hope yuh number eh turn out too low

Throw de dice, girl, throw!
Like yuh fingers freeze, yuh cahn let go

Throw de dice, girl, throw!
It look like is 'fraid yuh 'fraid to know

Throw de dice, girl, throw!
Wha' yuh say, yuh eh believe in such chupidness?

Yuh say we hol' we fate in we own han'
Is we own fault dat we cahn get on
We bog dung by too much superstition

Blame de dice when tings dohn turn out like we plan
We hah to fin' de will to free weself
Leave de pas' behind, it dead an' gone but
let de memory give we de strength to push
fuh wha' we want
An' if dey try to pin we back against de wall
take tuh de street so dey know we eh makin' joke
Man to man we fightin' fuh we rights
Is bottle, stick and brick fuh some ah we
Gun an' tank fuh we sister an' we brudder
in other countries

Is dah wha' yuh say?!!

Throw de dice, girl, throw!
Fling de ting out de dam' window

Long Road To Nowhere

Distances between
a marginal error
I don't want to be
inside my head
sharing space with
this stranger who
is not
Who is
the visible presence
of all things
unseen but felt
in the dark wells
of your mind
taken too far
across the line
too far
too far
The wall does not hide
the presence on the
other side if
you have bricked in
emptiness. The
object from which
you tried to hide
is already safe
          safe
          safe
          safely
locked inside
your head
Kentish Town Road one blast filled steaming image
cut by heat waves
later
Zebras and gorillas
What was I doing there?
I don't know
It was all so long
          ago
Zebras and gorillas
          cut
Zebras and gorillas
          cut
Zebras and gorillas
          cut
writhing the absurd myth
nourishing the foolish, brainless

fat bellied narrow-minds who
like it that way
Hard lines
        cut
uneasily
Kentish Town Road hot nightmare
        cut
the body
            His
What was I doing there?
I don't know
It was all so long ago
like yesterday
This stranger sharing space
inside my head
Walk easy, lady
If you can
If you dare
Walk
Dare you?
While he –
Kentish Town Road
nightmare image
People
No
milling ants
preoccupation intent
Saturday
shopping fray
walking between
to cross
why cross
the road
which separates
one from the
other?
always
the road
crossed the road
to the other side
Walking up
Waking up
Open your eyes, lady
and look
Open your eyes you
complacent
superior
bitch

and look
see where the road leads
See where the road leads?
All your life you have been
walking
with your eyes down
but for the first
time
you saw
the stranger who
still shares
your brain
        cut
the poetry
You were walking down Kentish Town Road when you saw –
        No
hold it
it dampens
the fever
controls
the anger
        cut back
to oasis
Fertile
This dry
barren dust
which swept
itself along
the pavement
of that
choked London
road
walking up
  and
waking up
to see you
coming down
up
down
        cut
the image
        cut
the excuses
        cut
the crap
        cut
but you can't
not the pain
ever

Why does it live?
Jesus Christ
why
does he haunt me
still
share my brain?
This stranger
            cut
getting closer
            cut
getting deeper
realization
sledge hammer
between the eyes
            cut
from the trunk
to the ankle
the drug
which
mutilates
the drug
which takes
fingers hands
arms
took
legs
stumbled over him
caught
his eyes
caged
trapped at the zebra
throw back
which walks on hands
because there are
no legs
throw back
to the other side
on hands because
there are no legs
throw back to me
across the zebra
crossing
naked to the waist
turn away
trunks
no legs
just feet
trunk perfect
perfect

dark tan
BLACK
muscle arms
strength
through walking
          cut
no legs
                    balancing on palms
                    of hands build
                    muscles

                    let the ad men
                    use that one
trapped
turned once
I
who strut
to see
him
cross
recross
the road
                    Does it all the time dear
                    spends all day just crossing and
                    recrossing that bloody road
                    So would you you stupid old hag
          cut
Cross the boundary
There is none
I
who strut
watched him
The eyes
met mine
Damn him
and me
seeped into my brain
The Jungle in
Kentish Town
Zebras and gorillas
And Sweet Jesus don't we face
enough problems just being black
without THAT
Throw back
put his load on me
Bash your head against the wall
until your brains splash their
understanding
Bang your head against the bars

until
they bend
strength in arms
enough space to let
us both
through
The drug which cuts
          cut
the will for him
to walk like a man
Still
he crosses and
recrosses the road
gorilla on a zebra's back
The myth which makes
them smile
hide their mouths
behind their hands
took me to the limit
and now he shares
my brain
I want to move aside
and give him space
This stranger
mutilated
monstrous
helpless
I carry him on
my back
His eyes
touched mine
trapped
on a zebra crossing
Two decades
of being caged
  b
    u
      t
this gun
looking at them
will serve
us
both

Dying In The Street

Megga
your child dying in the street!

We ran to my brother
not yet sixteen
the men with guns
stood at his side
Megga
hugged him
rocked him
tried to kiss life
back into those still lips
saw the desperation
still mirrored in eyes
which would not close
Megga
held her head
her wail was a cry
of the centuries
rising and clawing
the highest pinnacles
of anguish
then ebbing away
to mere grief
only to be picked up
in some other womb
only to reverberate
in the bosom
of some other woman
who sees her reflection
long and clear
on a blade
random and merciless

The halter to strangle the instincts
Your child dying in the street!
Megga
knows
I stand firm
when I say
it will never
come to
my
door

Midnight Without Pity

Judas
take my hand
let us go from here
down into the valley
Keep your hood tight
about your neck
I do not want to see
your face
and if you still remember
the bitter taste
to know
you never stood a chance
or had a choice
against a destiny
which held you
manipulated you
rejected you
then teach me
teach me
teach me how
to count the silver
and forget the cost
for I am
Black
and I am
Angry
my name is
Midnight
Without
Pity

Missionary

You witnessed nothing
I hid it from
your apathy
When you turned your back
you should have
opened your eyes
but you walk like thunder
Cracks
span
your every space
I could not
follow
your lead
So you left me
lame
in your thoughts
and rearranged
trodden
beneath your morality
Before you reach the edge
turn once
and scan the sky
the eagle
with a broken wing
will be me

Another Stab At The Wishing Well

I wish
            I was immuned
I wish
            I was safe
from the whips and daggers
which flay me without mercy
I wish
            I was hard and sturdy
like a rock set deep in the ocean
I wish
            I was so strong
that nothing could budge or disturb me
Imbedded deep in the sand
waves would wash over me
soothed by the sea
I would close my eyes
lulled and appeased
I would go to sleep
Oblivious to ruin
I would sleep
forever

Hole In The Wind

Autumn
    like a dull exclamation mark
and I
    with a restless hunger
kicking dead leaves
this way and that
You must have thought me
mad
At any rate
a little strange
I sensed you by my side
As ancient as the trees
Eyes
    like ice
    like fire
There were times when
I could not
look into them
You would lean
    on my arm
and on days when nothing
made much sense
I would lean
    on your wisdom
I missed you
I waited
in vain
You would smile and say
        There's a hole in the wind
        We go through it
        on our way
        to something
        or other
I will make an arrow
from the first flowers
of spring
and shoot it into space
It will write
your epitaph

Like Dogs

They hounded us like dogs
Until we took to our knees
Until we were ashamed to turn
our faces
towards the light
Our bellies crawling
in the mud
Hearts like festering wounds
festering wounds like cankers
opening opening getting wider
And oh God
the stench
I can taste myself rotting
I can still smell the afterbirth
and
my
dead
child
I can still see the fumes
from the iron
feel it
hot
hot
hot
red hot
The pain
of roasting flesh

Molten lava running through my brain

Black flesh
like me

Forget?!
Believe me
If I could
I damn well would

Going Home

When I was sixteen
you held a mirror
to the light
Now that I am
past twenty-one
you may have turned it
to the wall
Every line was put there
by me
or someone like me
I know that
When I come home
you will kill
the fatted calf?!
(You would do better
to keep it
firm
to its mother's side!)
but put sackcloth
and ashes by the roadside
a razor
to shave my head
then leave me
and I will do
my duty
by you

The Last Goodbye

We sip coffee
From time to time
I glance at your face
You are already a long way
away
Whatever plans you have made
do not include me
I am in barren, hostile land
There is a dryness in my throat
which no salive can soothe
I rise to my feet
My legs are brittle and stiff
The drought has set in
You drain your cup
unconcerned
I turn at the door
waiting
for just one
word
but you say
nothing
and silence is the saddest
word
of all
They brought you home
broken and
still
I could not bring myself
to look on
you
but as I laid
your wreath
and walked away
I knew
that if bitter memories
were the only fruit
I could bear
from all the love that I had
for you
that there might well
be no next
time
and
I have yet
to go back
on my word

He Is My Brother

They ridiculed me
said
You can't understand how it feels!
How could YOU possibly know?!
then
they left me
to brood
on their scorn

It is true
that I was not
born in this place
where a man
must
spend his life
clinging
to the shadows
I am shielded
by circumstances
But he
and I
are one
Chained
by the link
which binds us
HE
IS
MY
BROTHER
His
SWEAT
is my
tears

Circle Of Thorns

There is a ring which shines brightly
It is the answer to our prayers
I am not afraid

There is a ring of rusty iron
which grates along concrete
until your blood crawls
And
I have seen
I have seen
I have seen the young willow
sink beneath the waves
    beneath the waves
    beneath the hand which does not
replenish
So
when they ask
For whom the bell tolls?
Tell them
    Male black aged nineteen
    Female black aged seventeen
Two faces
in
a storm

Rainbow Dancer

I held you
through a fine rainbow scan
checking out every prism
of light
trapped in its mesh
absorbing
rejecting
wafting colours
to the breeze
Blue denim faded
against your tobacco skin
Beautiful!
You were beautiful
I couldn't have made you
closer to perfection
if I had chisled you
        moulded you
        fashioned you
after my own whim
Stirred by the music
you swayed
as in a trance
gently
slowly
Your eyes shut out the world
and me
I needed you
In desperation
I blew you love messages
They clung to the threads
They lay trapped in their web
None reached you
so I touched you through a veil
stroked you with music
Our bodies moving in unision
undulating on a calm
synchronized like a reflection
I danced with you
in a rainbow mist
until
you faded
with the night

Thursday, February 10th

Now that it is over
in theory
and the dust has settled
so that my footprints
are little more than
vague
impressions in the sand
I see they lead
as always
to my brick wall
I may need to turn
and face it
once again
Like some of my sign
I tried to
batter
my way through
I broke my horns
I bled
So
If for once
You see my tears
do not comfort me
let them flow
They are not acid
They will not burn
my face

Just give me time
to fix my smile
and damn
them all
again!

Celine

Time is not on my side
Celine
It has eroded me until
I am less
than a grain of sand
Celine nods
she understands
I can see from her face
that she is ill
but she will not speak
of it
Am I going to lose you
too
Celine?
I take her hand
it is cold
I thought she would shrink from me
but she did not
I search for words
which will bring
comfort
to us both
but I find
none
so we sit
hand in hand
in silence
It is summer
I feel lazy but
I am not relaxed
Celine
will be gone
before morning
dragged from her bed
by the demon
who will take her
and fling her
along the highways
of the possessed
leaving
me
nothing

Eden Revisited

The country hums
sweet sounds of recognition
so gentle
so soft
It's nice to know I can go back
The scent of all the things
I hold close
melt into a fusion
of delight
and my mind grows dizzy with pleasure
So nice to know I can go back
Shades of reunion
like the wisp of a smile
play smoothly
on a background
of ebony silk
I hold the threads between my fingers
They are safe
They will never fray
I will take them with me
when I go
and
in Oxford
on a cold
grey afternoon
I swore
I saw
    a humming-bird
        fly
            past
                my
                    window